...to live in this world

poems by

Judy Hood

Finishing Line Press
Georgetown, Kentucky

...to live in this world

Copyright © 2021 by Judy Hood
ISBN 978-1-64662-693-9 First Edition
All rights reserved under International and Pan-American Copyright Conventions. No part of this book may be reproduced in any manner whatsoever without written permission from the publisher, except in the case of brief quotations embodied in critical articles and reviews.

ACKNOWLEDGMENTS

I am ever and always appreciative to Julia Gregg for lifelong inspiration and trust, to Jamia Dixon, Annie Dixon, Vicki Snyder, and my dear friend Frances Mitchell for insight and intuition, to my Flamingos for Love and Light.

Thank you to Maureen Seaton, Mia Leonin, Diana Abu-Jaber, Evelina Galang, and Melissa Burley for your perceptive *ways of seeing* and eidetic ways of saying, to Joy and John for believing and enduring, and to Don for Pablo.

Title inspiration-Pablo Neruda, *Absence and Presence*
Inspiration for "Self Portrait with Protest"—Maureen Seaton

Italicized words in "Mission Dolores," "Thanking Joe," "Seed Harvest," and *"I have an Eye..."* are quoted from Dylan Thomas, Hunter S. Thompson, Boris Pasternak, and Mia Leonin.

Publisher: Leah Huete de Maines
Editor: Christen Kincaid
Cover Art: Judy Hood
Section Photos: Judy Hood
Author Photo: Kerri-Leanne Taylor
Cover Design: Elizabeth Maines McCleavy

Order online: www.finishinglinepress.com
also available on amazon.com

Author inquiries and mail orders:
Finishing Line Press
PO Box 1626
Georgetown, Kentucky 40324
USA

Table of Contents

Morning rips my heart out 1

Mission Dolores 2

Thanking Joe 3

I can't leave 6

Rain 7

I want it to be you 8

From my balcony 9

Under the Tamarind 10

On the Back Porch 11

Seed Harvest 13

Wild Guava Receipt 15

Gathering Blackberries 19

Self Portrait with Protest 20

Blue Hydrangeas 21

Amsterdam where I've never been 22

The Painting, Mehmet Guleryuz 23

I have an eye on my neighbor's feisty Palomino 24

for my father, who taught me to love words,
their meaning and their music
for the sons of my heart who came to live in this world

"...despite all that falls away from us...
the Light between us holds..."
Julia Hightower Gregg

Morning rips my heart out

I gasp to see it at my feet, broken into shards of memory
on the tile.
So sudden.
Gusts grab up the pieces, hurling them to the scudding clouds,
to the tamarind tops,
to the hawk's eye.

Slinging bits of plasma on the canvas dome,
chasing silver wing tips, soaring
south to purple sea,
west to emerald canyon,
north to cantaloupe moon,
suspended in the charcoal night.

Swirling in the cyclone,
spinning out on the fury of the chimes,
into echoes of rocking rails.
Wails and cataracts
bear witness to the ambush.
Savage shock.

Oh! shattered heart,
buried so far down and deep,
in mausoleum and sarcophagus sealed.
How could this be?

It was only Morning waiting
just outside this door.

Heart, fist of muscle, merely,
hands fly to rescue,
to protect,
but come away blood-stained.

I stoop to gather pieces that remain
and zip them helter skelter back inside the parts of me
that breathe and lift and walk and bear the weight,
still.

Mission Dolores

Girl with jet hair,
silk and veil,
inky as the night sky,
shivers in the chasm
at the vortex of the V
roof beams cut out of ebony,
moonbeams seek,
slipping down walls of the well
with no end.

Girl, just like the One I used to know,
moving like Him
in the world,
against the world,
for the world.

For the love of god
how could you do this?

Snatch away the dawn,
hush the dragon's song,
dam the river's spring,
turn fire to ice.

She *does not go gentle*
into grief's glacier,
rebels against its cold infinity,
gathers all the points of light
that tremble overhead
and rises to her mourning dance.

Thanking Joe

Mango blossoms,
somewhere between blaze and ash, rust and burnished copper.

In between.

Aren't we always there?
on the way to, coming from.
The gumbo limbo rattles its new leaves,
tiny castanets at the tips of its snakeskin branches.
Bougainvillea waterfalls cascade purple and magenta.
Bees hum, vibrating in the ecstasy of intoxication.

I am drawn as they are,
seduced by hue and honey.

I would not be here now if not for Joe.

A study in contrasts,
he scared me just a little.
Long hair pulled back into a hippie pony tail,
college banner on his lawn.
Dead head painted on his Harley,
walking four perfectly groomed Yorkies.
On the weekend, he would come around the hibiscus to offer water
 when I challenged the rocks at the property edge,
shovel against coral, scraping across his quiet Sunday reverie.

But two days ago he turned around his brand new pickup truck,
offered to cut back the vines I pruned
as they curled over his fence into our back yard.

Oh no. Please don't cut them. You know we love the green.
You know we love the color.

His bougainvillea painted our mornings and brush stroked our evening golden hour.
We thanked him for that once with a bottle of Dom.
We thanked him every day.

The call came when I was outdoors, rescuing yellow oleander from strangling wood rose,
escaping into the wild profusion of palms and avocados, blossoms and seeds.
Tangled vines and leaves cushioned my collapse.
Just yesterday…just moments ago…just now.
Heading home on his motorcycle, clear of the Stretch.
Truck turned into him, never slowed down.

The Edge. T*he edge is still out there. Or maybe it's In.*
When the time comes, do we really get to *choose between Now and Later?*

I can't leave

Honey light lingers,
brushes green-gold on the Rangoon leaves.
Lavender myrtle blossoms
dance with Frangipani partners
to music the breeze makes high in the palms,
the birds make, calling families home,
the chimes make and remake,
notes ringing round and round,
spiraling.

Day goes down;
routine calls.
But I can't leave.

I want to bury my face in
parsley and basil and thyme,
in spearmint and bee balm and garlic.

I want to walk the tomato rings one more time,
visit my Citrines and my Galahads,
catch my breath in their cleansing scent.

Admire the heap of vines and branches,
evidence of sweaty, salty hours of clipping and carrying.

Look one last time for a mango
dropped from our neighbor's tree
across the fence,
before the squirrels can claim it.

Take it home for sweet supper.

Rain

is out there,
skipping on roof ridges,
tickling the tamarind,
keeping its distance,
playing hide and seek
in the tomatoes, turning.
I can see their blush from here.

I sit on the edge,
my toes just inside
the drip line.
It is beginning to feel
like home page, now.
On the edge.

Rain
sounds as if it is running on tiptoes
in the backyard,
next to the wet wood fence,
but it is dripping on me
and on the page,
and off the roof,
into the arugula,
onto the terrace and tile
on the other side of this invisible curtain.

Circles swim together.
Venn diagrams float everywhere.
Griffin guards the door.

I want it to be you

    The chimes your mother sent,
    singing, sighing, when not a whisper of a breeze
    touches the bougainvillea
    or the petrea's star flower.

I want it to be you.
    The blue jay perched
    so singular and strange,
    his head turned to stare-
    locking eyes with me.

I want it to be you.
    The light flickering overhead
    like Morse code, insistent,
    inexplicable, repeating, blink…
    blink, blink, blink…blink.

I want it to be you.
    Salt at the margarita's rim,
    bite of the arugula, homegrown,
    bee's hum in the lingaro,
    its fragrance soft as cattleya's breath.

I want it to be you.
    Dancing in the yard,
    smoking on the balcony,
    laughing in the fire's light,
    spinning vinyl in your bar.

You.
    in Selene's song,
    in the guava glaze,
    in the key lime recipe,
    in the ink and in the pen.

I want it to be you,
    coming over.

From my balcony

I photograph
the Poincianas,
text them to my mother.

Do you see them?
One, two,
Blushing.

Maybe you could come for a Poinciana walk.
You know how many Royals are in my neighborhood.
We could walk 10 feet apart in the Park
Or parallel on either side of the street.

We could talk through our masked mouths.
We could talk with our eyes.
And listen
To the trees.

Under the Tamarind

When she rounds the corner at the back porch landing,
I tuck the mask loops around my ears.
Separate, we walk to the Tamarind tree,
where lawn chairs wait eight feet apart.

Her mask is pink and patterned,
pleated and soft, like the Frangipani petals
that drop their feathers on her shoulders.
Her yoga leggings wrap like pretzels on the iron cross-hatch
where she clips her keys and balances a water bottle.

She hasn't been inside my house in nearly a year,
and I've not been in hers,
       not for birthday omelettes
       or Christmas tea cakes
       or guava-jelly-making day.

Today, she has mown her avocado grove and done the
dreaded marketing where people
       stand too close and
       argue with the cashier and
       let their masks slip down around their chins.

Today, I have taken a little orchid to my neighbor's door
and sobbed to see it standing open beyond the screen.
       Open to the memory of the Carambola.
       Open to the whisper of the oak's sigh.
       Open to the lacey light.

Today, the painter next door began his work
before my morning coffee.
       Singing in a voice I understood.
       Singing in a language I couldn't speak.
       Singing as if last night's fiesta would never end.

       Free and lusty and fearless.

On the Back Porch

I stand at the back door on the Hurricane Porch,
next to the water jug and Granny's old laundry basket
with the last of my son's seed collections and his dog's rock and Kong.

I stand here with my cell phone
and my garden gloves
and my clippers
and my sunshade
and sing James Taylor in my mind.

Sweet dreams and flying machines in pieces on the ground.

How many hours have I stood here,
paced these tiles,
crossed and criss-crossed
these few square feet?

The place where groceries land in green plastic bags
before the alcohol wipe-down.
The place for laundry sorting: lights, darks, delicates, heavies, his, mine.
The place where orchids dance and wait and wait to finally find their home.

I stand here.
Write down everything.
Go out.

Plant seeds.

Seed Harvest

I lace up my yard shoes and find my clippers
still nestled in the gloves,
curved into claws, stiffened by the dirt I never wash away,
and head out across the grass, crackling, crunching
in the sun that bakes what escaped the frost's burn,
into the cool quiet of the oaks and avocados and palms.
Chamaedorea seifrizii.
He always *called each thing by its right name.*

I remember when he planted them,
baby bamboo palms, under leafy branches of the avocado trees,
so he could water them and feed them
and mow between the rows.
And after all the pears were picked, the Donnies and
the Simmonds and the Monroes,
we would pull the seeds.

I was a young mother then, and while my baby slept,
I would grade them,
dragging the seeds across a screen, sifting out the chaff and culls,
scooping them into burlap sacks, stripping the blue-black berries
from brilliant orange stems,
rubbing, rolling jet beads under my fingertips.

The old man's been gone so long now,

but I can see him still, bent leg propped, eyeglasses on his nose,
turning pages of the seed catalogs, comparing heights-
pear to palm-calculating picking seasons,
and, of course, the profit.

Now, wood rose and philodendron choke his avocados,
insinuate themselves among the fronds.
His sons never top the trees or mow the grove,
much less come around.

.

His grandson crosses the country to wrestle vines,
cut away strangler figs,
burn dead wood in a bonfire that silhouettes his torso
against the night.

It's not exactly what the old man had in mind,
hunched over his Royal typewriter, pecking out the seed orders
and contemplating his will.

And I.
I think about seeds all the time.
I covet them, dangling like blonde dreadlocks
over my neighbor's fence.
I see them swing in heavy necklaces of coral and crimson.
I collect them in cracked clay pots, in bowls, in baskets,
in pockets.
I line them up on windowsills.
I wake up in the night, dreaming of the seeds.

They hide in the fans like beaded dangles
flashing on flame fingers.
They fill up my cupped hands like grape clusters,
ripened for the press.
They swell my shoulder sack with promise-laden stems.

As sunset spills its mango, guava, muscadine across the sky,
my heart goes on,
pulling seeds.

Wild Guava Receipt

He planted three wild guavas raised from seed.
One to the south of the five acres,
just outside their bedroom window,
behind the brick fish pond with its coral rock waterfall
and beneath the towering Sapodilla,
whose fuzzy skinned fruit vied with smooth, waxy orbs
for sticky, syrupy, sweetness.

Another grew at the north boundary between pink grapefruit
and sea grape,
beside the only orchid house left standing,
next to his workshop, where rusty lawn rockers
and saggy-bottomed cane straight-backs clustered in the cross
breeze among his tools, and saws, and tractors.

The last point of his *guayaba* triangle rose due east
from the back porch,
a surprise in the line of avocados and seed palms,
close to the walkway that circled their land,
the path where she pushed the grandbaby's stroller,
where she could walk in her little high heel pumps
after a day of teaching, to gather limes for the evening's
sweet tea.

It was no wonder that the guava was her favorite.
Plump and sunny, its ripe skins looked like oils
in her still life paintings.
Bursting open, rosy flesh puzzled the senses,
curious, exotic, mysterious.
She would make jam from her calamondins,
ambrosia from the yard tree,
guava shells to serve with cream cheese and Cuban crackers.
But he made guava jelly.

With pots boiling over, pulp and seed-filled
bundles of cheesecloth
suspended from copper pots overhead,
guava nectar, lime juice, and sugar sticking to every counter-top
and floor tile,
the kitchen was off limits to everyone else.
What joy in the jar at breakfast, and in the buttered
biscuit at dinner,
and in the memory.

We guarded the old-timer's recipe.
But in all the years since he's been gone,
we could never make jelly in his kitchen.
Syrup refused to slip off the spoon in shimmering sheets,
or it would harden into tar in the cooling jar.
We had to find another jelly kitchen,
so she never went without.

This summer, the ground fairly bubbled beneath the trees,
and the whole place hummed with bees.
We took it as an omen,
collecting in buckets, baskets, shirt hems, and pockets
all the fruit that birds and bugs and squirrels did not find first.

We filled her freezer, then filled another,
certain there would be time and time
for jelly making on Sunday afternoons, when dog days passed.

But fall overtook the summer.
Her spoonful of guava would often go untouched
alongside the scrambled eggs she requested every meal
but did not eat.
Care squeezed all the hours from our days
before we could set stainless pots to gurgling
and silver ladles to stirring.
Before we could pour captured sunlight into quilted jars.

Now I walk the property among the trees he planted.
The guavas are split and splintered like his family,
with limbs stretching up from shattered centers,
brought low by strangling invaders,
blighted by some insidious smut.

I touch the skin of branches bent like his arthritic leg,
smooth, hairless, liver spotted, cool like polished marble,
frozen in a perpetual bend, the way he propped it up
on the tractor
with my boy seated on his knee,
so he could reach out from his mowing machine
and pluck guavas from the sky.

Gathering Blackberries

When my mother took my hand as we walked up the hill,
past the cows munching grass, crunching clover
under cotton clouds,
past the broken fence where Holly Berry
had somehow got into the garden
and helped herself to the cucumbers,
I didn't think she would be leading me to a cliff's edge,
just beyond the creek.
I only knew we were going to pick blackberries.

I remember licking the memory of syrup at the corners of my mouth,
anticipating sweet, juicy blackberries waiting for me.
Help yourself, my mother said, pointing to the bush,
and I reached out to pluck the plump ripeness.
Never heeding the needles hidden in the fuzzy leaves.
Never hearing the bees' whir.

Self Portrait with Protest

Justify.
When I lived under the lapis shadows of the Black Forest,
every day I hiked along the river, crossed the market's cobbles
to study at the University. Saving streetcar fare
guaranteed a trip across the Alps. I sang Edelweiss in Austria,
sipped schnapps in Munich, shivered in Red Square,
all because I could survive on black bread and
tomatoes and wear the same shoes for a year.

Life felt rich, living free like that,
responses simple, honest, good.
Reality challenged a silly girl's dream,
peace of mind stolen with the hand bag.
The attacker only took the room key,
left passport and virginity intact.

But signs in Le Havre condemned me for a murderer.
Le American.
What mattered tears and judgment when
napalm torched the forest and hoses blasted marching Truth?
While my flag flew in strips and tatters,
I drank my first beer, isolate in the riot,
Star-dancer in Berlin.

Blue Hydrangeas
after Ntozake Shange

I live in blue
hydrangeas, the ones we passed
in the cul-de-sac at the bottom of the
eucalyptus clean hill,
where dachshunds saunter through the park, chase runaway balls
and blowing leaves.

I live in blue
hydrangeas turned to tissue paper silver
on their stems, promising resurrection,
whispering of all the nights in fog and chill
they have endured
and all the days of light and warmth embraced.

I live in blue
hydrangeas that nod and wave
as children spill out
into angled sun on slanted streets
and gasp, Oh, blue! Is it real?
Baby blue, sky blue, Bay blue,
cornflower, plumbago,
Copenhagen blue.

I live in blue
hydrangeas, spiraling in the mall,
looking, for all their honesty,
like antique French lace-tops, tied in silken ribbon,
sewn by the milliner's needle
into Miriam's hat band.

I live in blue
hydrangeas, admired in the market,
their cost too dear
to take home and plant
under the window,
where Dylan sings,
all *tangled up in blue.*

Amsterdam where I've never been

It is Sunday. Streets stretch broad and clean, open to all possibilities. Bicycles roll by, silent. Dogs tug against their leashes to sniff the curb. On the sidewalk, a café invites us for a coffee, for a smoke, for a moment, for this moment we have promised each other.

Shadow and dancing light, filtering through the elms, say Stay. Spring snow blossoms dust a spell and the text screen goes dark. Put the calendar, the itinerary on hold. Edvard and Vincent will wait for us. Bells chime from steeples rising along the boulevard, echo back from apartment buildings and storefronts and balconies. But no hymns float from open doors. The congregation sleeps.

Blue and silver skies, cloudless, calming, crystal, float close enough to dip a breath, deep and slow, without fear that the seconds too soon will evaporate, that they will collapse, and we will find ourselves again on opposite sides of a continent, opposite sides of time. Suspended on the same side of hopes and histories and loves lost. Only this ice air, this cup, this curve of cream and curl of ash and scent of bloom breathe benediction.

The Painting, Mehmet Guleryuz

Eye sacs droop and skin drips
down like candle wax. Earlobes slip
beneath his rumpled collar.
From behind, she presses powdery cheek
against the wing tip of his shoulder,
but her chin lifts away.
Coquette.
Ringlets drop from their cottony crown
to frame her Baby Bye-Lo face,
bisque glaze, crazed.
Lips, tint faded, turn to brush an occasional
patch of wool atop liver-spotted pate;
arms make a circle 'round sunken chest and sagging belly.

They will not say its name out loud.
But memory cries for all the nights they kept each other safe,
in fern forest and canyon,
on mountain ridge and coral reef,
stars flung, comets crashing.

No matter that these feet that walked where angels landed
now splay like broken branches that no boot can lace,
that breath wheezes a decay no honey can sweeten,
and eagle eyes strain against the Falconer's hood.

No matter.

They go on.

I have an eye on my neighbor's feisty palomino

Cut from a cloth that wears well,
I was born to walk, not ride.
Run, not fly.
But today
I scoop up sugar cubes
and corn and fill
the pockets of my apron.

Wear jeans beneath my skirts,
mask leather with lace,
braid my hair with ribbons
and wrap my throat with beads.

The Papi won't notice.
The hens that cluck and scratch and peck
will only see the tomatoes I drop for them.

When the bell tolls
and heads bow and hands fold,
I will blow out my candle on the altar.
I will fly
without saddle or
halter or bridle
or boot.

Judy Hood holds an MFA in Creative Writing from the University of Miami where she teaches Writing Studies and Visual Rhetoric. She has received recognition for her poetry and prose from the Robert Frost Heritage House Poetry Festival and Pirate's Alley Faulkner Society, an award for Best Start Fiction from *Glimmertrain*, and publication of her stories in *The Miami Herald* and *The Southern Quarterly*. As recipient of the Andrew Mellon CREATE grant she researched and wrote *Attic Treasure: Flagler's Dream Train*. For five summers she has co-hosted Summer Soulstice, a Writers' Workshop, whose participants have aired their stories on StoryCorps E-NPR and published *Sheltering*, a collection of their Summer 2020 writing, painting, and photography.

Her first book of poetry *…to live in this world*, connects deep loss to shared grief, experiences the living, breathing moment with acute awareness of its ephemeral fragility, and reflects on the paths that have brought her to connect profoundly with the natural world. Her poetry resonates with the soulful braiding of wonder and pain, of the intimate personal and the essential elemental.

www.ingramcontent.com/pod-product-compliance
Lightning Source LLC
Chambersburg PA
CBHW050822090426
42737CB00022B/3474